FINANCIAL FREEDOM

I0446594

HOW TO RETIRE YOUNG, RICH, AND HAPPY

JOY DANIELS

Copyright © 2023 by Joy Daniels

TABLE OF CONTENT

INTRODUCTION

Welcome to the transformative journey towards financial freedom with my latest Amazon book, "Financial Freedom: How to Retire Young, Rich, and Happy." In an era where the pursuit of a fulfilling and liberated life is more crucial than ever, this book serves as your comprehensive guide to achieving not just monetary success, but a holistic sense of prosperity and joy.

In a world dominated by financial complexities, this book distils the essence of strategic wealth-building, offering practical insights, actionable steps, and time-tested principles that pave the way to early retirement. Drawing from a wealth of financial expertise, I unravel the secrets of investment, savings, and smart money management, guiding you through a roadmap that empowers you to break free from the shackles of financial stress and retire on your terms.

"Financial Freedom" goes beyond mere financial advice; it delves into the psychology of money, helping you cultivate a mindset that fosters abundance and a genuine sense of well-being. The narrative is woven with real-life examples, success stories, and cautionary tales, creating a compelling and relatable narrative that resonates with readers from all walks of life.

This book is not just about accumulating wealth; it's about creating a life where your money works for you, affording you the luxury of time, experiences, and the freedom to pursue your passions. Whether you're just starting on your financial journey or looking to optimize your existing wealth, "Financial Freedom" provides a roadmap that is both accessible and empowering.

Embark on this enriching voyage towards financial liberation, where you retire not just financially secure but also enriched with the priceless treasures of a fulfilled and happy life. It's time to rewrite your financial story and embrace a future that is abundant, joyful, and truly liberated.

CHAPTER 1: THE FOUNDATION OF FINANCIAL FREEDOM

Welcome to the cornerstone of your financial journey – Chapter 1: The Foundation of Financial Freedom. In this pivotal section, we delve deep into the bedrock principles that underpin the quest for financial liberation. Understanding that wealth is not solely about numbers on a balance sheet, we embark on a journey to explore the intricate interplay between mindset, goals, and the psychology of money.

This chapter opens with an exploration of the often underestimated but critically important element – the Psychology of Money. We unravel the emotional nuances that influence financial decisions, providing you with insights that will empower you to make informed and rational choices. Building upon this understanding, we then delve into the cultivation of a Strong Financial Mindset, a key asset on the road to prosperity. It's not just about the money; it's about how you think about and relate to it.

As we progress, we guide you through the process of Defining Your Financial Goals and Objectives. This step is foundational – a roadmap that will shape your financial decisions and actions. By setting clear intentions, you pave the way for a purpose-driven and fulfilling financial journey.

Get ready to embark on a transformative exploration that goes beyond the numbers. The Foundation of Financial Freedom is not just about accumulating wealth; it's about nurturing a mindset and setting goals that align with your values, leading you towards a life of abundance, joy, and true financial liberation. Let's lay the groundwork for a future where your money serves as a tool for happiness and fulfilment.

- The Psychology of Money

The Psychology of Money is a profound and intricate aspect of personal finance that explores the emotional and behavioral dimensions of our relationship with money. Far beyond the mere numbers and transactions, our thoughts, feelings, and beliefs about money shape our financial decisions, habits, and ultimately, our financial well-being.

One key element of the Psychology of Money is the understanding of individual attitudes toward risk and reward. People vary widely in their tolerance for financial risk, and this is often influenced by personal experiences, cultural background, and psychological factors. Some individuals may be risk-averse, prioritizing the preservation of wealth, while others may be more inclined to take risks in pursuit of higher returns. Recognizing and understanding one's risk tolerance is crucial for making investment decisions aligned with one's comfort level.

Additionally, the concept of "money scripts" plays a significant role in the Psychology of Money. Money scripts are the beliefs and assumptions individuals hold about money, often formed in childhood based on observations of how their parents or caregivers handled finances. These scripts can be positive or negative, influencing financial behaviors. Unearthing and challenging limiting money scripts can be a transformative step toward healthier financial habits.

The Psychology of Money also encompasses the impact of societal and cultural influences on financial decision-making. Social norms, peer pressure, and societal expectations contribute to our financial choices, sometimes leading us to make decisions that may not align with our true values and goals. Understanding these external influences allows individuals to make more intentional and authentic financial decisions.

Moreover, emotions such as fear, greed, and impulse play a significant role in shaping financial behaviors. Recognizing the emotional aspects of financial decision-making enables individuals to develop emotional intelligence, making it easier to navigate challenges like market volatility and financial setbacks.

In essence, the Psychology of Money emphasizes that personal finance is not solely a numbers game; it is a deeply human experience. By understanding and addressing the psychological aspects of our financial lives, individuals can cultivate a healthier and more sustainable relationship with money, leading to greater financial well-being and fulfilment.

- Building a Strong Financial Mindset

Building a Strong Financial Mindset is a transformative process that involves cultivating a set of attitudes, beliefs, and behaviors that contribute to a positive and empowered relationship with money. A strong financial mindset is crucial for making informed decisions, setting and achieving financial goals, and ultimately achieving financial freedom. Here's a breakdown of the key steps in the process:

1. Self-Awareness:

- *Understand your current beliefs about money:* Reflect on your existing attitudes and beliefs about money. Identify any negative or limiting beliefs that may be hindering your financial growth.

- *Assess your financial habits:* Examine your spending, saving, and investing habits. Identify patterns that may be impacting your financial well-being.

2. Educate Yourself:

- *Financial literacy:* Invest time in increasing your financial knowledge. Understand basic financial concepts, investment strategies, and the principles of budgeting and saving.

- *Learn from experts:* Seek guidance from financial advisors, read books, attend workshops, and follow reputable financial blogs to gain insights and perspectives from experienced professionals.

3. Goal Setting:

- *Define clear financial goals:* Set specific, measurable, and realistic financial goals. Whether it's saving for a home, funding education, or achieving early retirement, having well-defined goals provides direction and motivation.

- *Break down goals into manageable steps:* Create actionable steps to achieve your financial goals. Breaking down larger objectives into smaller, achievable tasks makes the journey more manageable and less overwhelming.

4. Positive Visualization:

- *Envision financial success:* Practice positive visualization by imagining yourself achieving your financial goals. This helps reinforce a positive mindset and instils confidence in your ability to overcome challenges.

- *Focus on abundance:* Shift your mindset from scarcity to abundance. Acknowledge and appreciate the resources you have, fostering a positive outlook on your financial situation.

5. Adaptability and Resilience:

- *Embrace a growth mindset:* See challenges as opportunities for learning and growth. A growth mindset enables you to adapt to changing circumstances and view setbacks as temporary hurdles.

- *Develop resilience:* Understand that financial journeys have ups and downs. Cultivate resilience by learning from failures, adjusting your approach, and persisting in the pursuit of your financial goals.

6. Surround Yourself with Positivity:

- *Choose positive influences:* Surround yourself with individuals who share similar financial values and goals. Positive peer influence can provide encouragement and support on your financial journey.

- Limit exposure to negativity: Minimize exposure to financial negativity, whether it's from news, social media, or pessimistic individuals. Focus on constructive and optimistic information that aligns with your financial goals.

Building a Strong Financial Mindset is an ongoing process that involves self-reflection, continuous learning, and intentional actions. By adopting a positive and empowered mindset, individuals can navigate the complexities of personal finance with confidence and resilience.

- Defining Your Financial Goals and Objectives

Defining Your Financial Goals and Objectives is a crucial step in creating a roadmap for your financial journey. It involves clarifying your aspirations, values, and priorities, and setting specific, measurable targets that guide your financial decisions. The process is dynamic, requiring self-reflection, strategic planning, and periodic reassessment. Here's a breakdown of the key steps:

1. Self-Reflection:

 - *Identify Values and Priorities:* Consider what truly matters to you. Your financial goals should align with your values and priorities, whether it's homeownership, education, travel, or early retirement.

 - *Assess Short-Term and Long-Term Needs:* Distinguish between immediate financial needs and long-term aspirations. This helps in prioritizing goals and allocating resources accordingly.

2. Quantify Your Goals:

 - *Make Goals Specific and Measurable:* Vague goals are challenging to pursue. Define each goal with specificity and attach measurable criteria. For example, instead of "save for retirement," specify an amount and a target date.

 - *Categorize Goals:* Group goals into categories like short-term (1-3 years), medium-term (3-7 years), and long-term (7+ years). This segmentation aids in creating a timeline and allocating resources effectively.

3. Prioritize Goals:

- *Establish a Hierarchy:* Rank your goals based on importance and urgency. This hierarchy guides your financial planning and helps in allocating resources where they are needed most.

- *Consider Dependencies:* Recognize if achieving one goal is dependent on another. This understanding informs the sequencing of your goals.

4. Financial Assessment:

- *Evaluate Current Finances:* Assess your current financial situation, including income, expenses, assets, and liabilities. Understanding your financial baseline provides context for setting realistic goals.

- *Consider Risk Tolerance:* Evaluate your risk tolerance, especially for investment-related goals.

Some goals may involve more risk, such as investing in stocks, while others may require a more conservative approach.

5. Create an Action Plan:

- *Break Down Goals into Tasks:* Convert each goal into actionable steps. For example, if your goal is to eliminate credit card debt, tasks could include creating a budget, negotiating interest rates, and implementing a debt repayment strategy.

- *Allocate Resources:* Determine how much money and time you need to allocate to each goal. This includes regular contributions to savings or investment accounts.

6. Regular Review and Adjustment:

- *Periodic Assessment:* Regularly review your financial goals to ensure they remain relevant and aligned with your evolving priorities.

- *Adjust as Needed:* Life circumstances change, and your goals may need adjustment. Be flexible and willing to adapt your financial plan as needed.

Defining Your Financial Goals and Objectives is an ongoing, iterative process that evolves with your life journey. By setting clear, meaningful goals and regularly reassessing them, you create a financial roadmap that guides your decision-making and empowers you to achieve the financial future you desire.

CHAPTER 2: THE ART OF WEALTH ACCUMULATION

Welcome to the pivotal realm where financial dreams transform into reality – Chapter 2: The Art of Wealth Accumulation. In this chapter, we embark on a compelling exploration of the strategies, principles, and tactics that constitute the artistry of building wealth. Beyond the mere accumulation of assets, this section unveils the intricacies of smart saving, strategic investing, and the cultivation of sustainable streams of income.

As we delve into The Art of Wealth Accumulation, our journey begins with an in-depth exploration of Smart Saving Strategies for Long-Term Success. We unravel the nuances of effective budgeting, disciplined saving habits, and the power of compounding, laying the groundwork for a solid financial foundation.

From there, we transition into the dynamic landscape of Investing Wisely: Stocks, Bonds, and Real Estate. This section demystifies the world of investment, offering insights into asset allocation, risk management, and the art of crafting a diversified portfolio. Whether you are a seasoned investor or just starting, these principles will guide you in making informed and strategic investment decisions.

Our exploration culminates in Navigating the World of Passive Income Streams, where we unveil the transformative potential of generating income that works for you. From dividends and rental income to online ventures, we dissect the avenues that allow your money to labor on your behalf, creating a path to financial freedom and early retirement.

Get ready to embark on a journey that goes beyond conventional financial advice. The Art of Wealth Accumulation is not just about amassing riches; it's about mastering the principles that foster sustainable growth, resilience in the face of market volatility, and the creation of a financial landscape where your wealth aligns seamlessly with your life goals. Let the artistry of wealth accumulation guide you toward a future of financial abundance and prosperity.

- Smart saving Strategies for Long-Term Success

Smart Saving Strategies for Long-Term Success form the cornerstone of a sound financial plan, providing individuals with the tools to build a robust foundation for their future. The art of saving intelligently extends beyond mere budgeting; it encompasses disciplined habits, goal-oriented planning, and an understanding of the power of compounding. Here's an in-depth discussion of key elements within smart saving strategies:

1. **Budgeting with Purpose:**

- *Tracking and Categorizing Expenses:* Begin by meticulously tracking your spending. Categorize expenses to identify areas where you can cut back and redirect funds toward savings.

- Creating a Realistic Budget: Develop a budget that aligns with your financial goals. Ensure it allows for both necessary expenses and discretionary spending while leaving room for saving.

2. Emergency Fund Essentials:

- Building a Financial Safety Net: Allocate a portion of your savings toward an emergency fund. This fund acts as a financial safety net, providing a cushion for unexpected expenses or income disruptions.

- Determining the Right Size: Aim to save three to six months' worth of living expenses in your emergency fund. Adjust the target based on your circumstances, such as job stability and financial obligations.

3. Automated Savings and Pay Yourself First:

- *Setting up Automated Transfers:* Automate your savings by setting up regular transfers to your savings or investment accounts. This ensures consistency and makes saving a priority.

- *The "Pay Yourself First" Principle:* Prioritize saving by allocating a portion of your income to savings before addressing other expenses. This simple yet powerful principle establishes a savings habit as a primary financial commitment.

4. Harnessing the Power of Compounding:

- *Early Start and Consistent Contributions:* The earlier you start saving, the more time your money has to benefit from compounding. Consistent contributions over time amplify the compounding effect, leading to substantial long-term growth.

- *Exploring Compound Interest Investments:* Consider investment vehicles that offer compound interest, such as certain savings accounts, certificates of deposit (CDs), and investment portfolios. These options can enhance the growth of your savings over time.

5. Adjusting to Life Changes:

- *Flexible Saving Strategies:* Recognize that life circumstances change. Be prepared to adjust your savings strategies in response to changes in income, expenses, or financial goals.

- *Reassessing and Adapting:* Regularly reassess your financial situation and savings goals. Adjust your savings plan as needed to ensure it remains aligned with your evolving financial landscape.

6. Debt Management and Saving Simultaneously:

- *Prioritizing High-Interest Debt:* While saving is crucial, high-interest debt can erode your financial health. Prioritize paying down high-interest debt while still maintaining a savings routine to strike a balance between debt reduction and wealth accumulation.

In essence, Smart Saving Strategies for Long-Term Success involve a combination of disciplined budgeting, purposeful saving, and an understanding of the dynamics of time and compounding. By adopting these strategies, individuals not only secure their financial presence but also pave the way for a prosperous and resilient financial future.

- Investing Wisely: Stocks, Bonds, and Real Estate

Investing wisely in stocks, bonds, and real estate is a multifaceted process that requires a combination of financial knowledge, strategic planning, and a keen understanding of risk and return. This chapter explores the principles and considerations essential for making informed investment decisions.

1. **Educate Yourself:**

   - *Understand Investment Basics:* Before diving into the market, develop a foundational understanding of investment principles, including risk, return, diversification, and market dynamics.

- *Explore Different Asset Classes:* Gain insights into the characteristics of stocks, bonds, and real estate. Understand how each asset class functions, its historical performance, and its role in a diversified portfolio.

2. Define Your Investment Goals:

- *Short-Term vs. Long-Term Objectives:* Clarify whether you are investing for short-term goals (e.g., buying a house) or long-term objectives (e.g., retirement). Your investment horizon influences the choice of assets and risk tolerance.

3. Risk Tolerance and Asset Allocation:

- *Assess Your Risk Tolerance:* Understand your comfort level with risk. Different investments carry varying levels of risk, and your risk tolerance should align with your financial goals and emotional resilience.

- Strategize Asset Allocation: Diversify your portfolio by allocating assets across different classes—stocks for growth, bonds for income, and real estate for diversification. Adjust the allocation based on your risk tolerance and investment horizon.

4. Stock Market Strategies:

- Individual Stocks vs. Funds: Decide whether to invest in individual stocks or diversified funds. Individual stocks can offer high returns but also higher risk, while funds provide instant diversification.

- Research and Due Diligence: Conduct thorough research before investing in individual stocks. Understand the company's financials, industry trends, and growth potential.

5. Bond Investments:

- Types of Bonds: Explore various types of bonds, such as government bonds, corporate bonds, and municipal bonds. Each type carries its own risk and return profile.

- Yield and Maturity Considerations: Pay attention to bond yields and maturities. Higher yields often come with higher risk, and the maturity date affects the investment's sensitivity to interest rate changes.

6. Real Estate Investment:

- Rental Properties vs. Real Estate Investment Trusts (REITs): Decide between physical real estate investments like rental properties or the convenience of investing in REITs. Each option has its advantages and challenges.

- Market Research: Conduct thorough market research before investing in real estate. Consider factors like location, property appreciation potential, and rental market dynamics.

7. Continuous Monitoring and Adjustments:

- Stay Informed: Keep abreast of market trends, economic indicators, and changes in the regulatory environment. Regularly review your investment portfolio and assess whether it aligns with your goals.

- Rebalance Your Portfolio: Periodically rebalance your portfolio to maintain the desired asset allocation. Changes in market conditions or personal circumstances may warrant adjustments.

8. **Professional Guidance:**

- Consult Financial Advisors: Consider seeking advice from financial professionals who can provide personalized guidance based on your financial situation, goals, and risk tolerance.

- Stay Disciplined: Avoid making impulsive decisions based on short-term market fluctuations. Stick to your investment strategy and adjust it only after careful consideration.

Investing wisely is a dynamic process that involves continuous learning, adaptability, and a thoughtful approach to risk and reward. By following these principles, investors can navigate the complexities of the financial markets and work towards building a diversified and resilient investment portfolio.

- Navigating the World of Passive Income Streams

Navigating the World of Passive Income Streams is a transformative journey that empowers individuals to generate income with less active involvement, providing financial freedom and flexibility. This chapter explores the strategies and avenues for creating passive income, allowing individuals to build wealth and achieve financial independence. Here is a comprehensive discussion of the key elements in navigating passive income streams:

1. Understanding Passive Income:

 - *Definition and Types:* Passive income is money earned with minimal effort or active involvement. Explore various types of passive income, including dividends from stocks, rental income from real estate, interest from savings, and income from online businesses.

2. Identifying Passive Income Opportunities:

- *Investing in Dividend-Paying Stocks:* Dividend stocks can provide a steady stream of passive income. Invest in well-established companies with a history of consistent dividend payments.

- *Real Estate Investments:* Generate passive income through rental properties or real estate crowdfunding platforms. Real estate can offer both rental income and potential appreciation.

- *Interest from Savings and Investments:* Explore high-yield savings accounts, certificates of deposit (CDs), and bonds that provide regular interest payments.

3. Creating Online Passive Income Streams:

- *Blogging and Content Creation:* Monetize a blog or YouTube channel through advertising, sponsored content, or affiliate marketing. Over time, well-established online platforms can generate passive income.

- Digital Products and Courses: Create and sell digital products, online courses, or e-books. Once developed, these products can continue to generate income with minimal ongoing effort.

- Affiliate Marketing: Promote products or services and earn a commission on sales generated through your referral links. This model leverages existing platforms and audiences.

4. **Automating Business Ventures:**

- E-commerce and Dropshipping: Set up an online store that utilizes dropshipping to minimize hands-on involvement in inventory management and shipping.

- Automated Online Businesses: Develop and automate online businesses that can generate income through e-commerce, digital products, or subscription models.

5. **Risk Management and Diversification:**

- Diversifying Income Streams: Avoid relying on a single source of passive income. Diversification

mitigates risks associated with changes in market conditions or the performance of specific investments.

- *Understanding Risks:* Be aware of the potential risks associated with different passive income streams. Real estate may be subject to market fluctuations, and online businesses may face challenges like changing algorithms or competition.

6. **Scaling Passive Income Ventures:**

- *Reinvestment Strategies:* Reinvest profits from passive income ventures to scale and grow your portfolio. This could involve acquiring additional rental properties, expanding online businesses, or diversifying investments.

- *Continuous Improvement:* Regularly evaluate and enhance your passive income strategies. Explore new opportunities and technologies to stay ahead in the evolving landscape.

7. Passive Income and Early Retirement:

- *Financial Independence and Retire Early (FIRE):* Passive income is often a key component of the FIRE movement, enabling individuals to achieve financial independence and retire early.

- *Creating a Sustainable Lifestyle:* Design a lifestyle that aligns with your passive income goals. Consider factors such as living expenses, travel, and leisure activities.

Navigating the World of Passive Income Streams requires a combination of creativity, strategic planning, and a commitment to continuous improvement. By diversifying income sources and leveraging various passive income opportunities, individuals can create a sustainable financial future that aligns with their goals and aspirations.

CHAPTER 3: MONEY MANAGEMENT MASTERY

Welcome to the transformative realm where financial control becomes an art, and strategic decisions pave the way to enduring prosperity – Chapter 3: Money Management Mastery. In this chapter, we delve into the essential skills and principles that empower individuals to master the intricacies of their financial landscape. Beyond the mere accumulation of wealth, this section unveils the art of smart budgeting, effective debt management, and the cultivation of resilience through the establishment of emergency funds.

As we embark on the journey of Money Management Mastery, our exploration begins with the creation and maintenance of a Budget That Works. Here, we unravel the secrets of disciplined spending, strategic saving, and the powerful impact of tracking every dollar. A budget, when wielded with mastery, becomes a tool for financial clarity, empowerment, and the realization of long-term goals.

Following this, we venture into the realm of Debt Elimination Strategies for Financial Freedom. From understanding the different types of debt to crafting a tailored repayment plan, this section equips you with the knowledge and techniques necessary to free yourself from the shackles of financial burdens. Debt management is not just about repayment; it's about reclaiming control and fostering a healthier financial future.

Our exploration culminates in the importance of Emergency Funds and the Power of Financial Resilience. In an unpredictable world, the ability to weather financial storms is paramount. Discover the art of building a financial safety net, ensuring that unexpected setbacks do not derail your journey to financial mastery.

Get ready to elevate your financial acumen to new heights. Money Management Mastery is not just about managing money; it's about mastering the art of strategic financial decision-making. It's about creating a resilient and empowered relationship with your finances, where each decision aligns with your long-term aspirations. Let the mastery of money management guide you toward a future of financial stability, security, and enduring success.

- Creating and Maintaining a Budget That Works

Creating and maintaining a budget that works is a fundamental aspect of effective money management. A well-crafted budget serves as a financial roadmap, providing clarity, discipline, and control over your spending and saving habits. Here's a comprehensive discussion of the process of creating and maintaining a budget that stands the test of financial challenges:

1. **Assess Your Financial Situation:**

  - *Income Evaluation:* Begin by determining your total monthly income. Include all sources of income, such as salaries, freelance work, and any additional streams.

  - *Expense Analysis:* Review your monthly expenses. Categorize them into fixed expenses (e.g., rent, mortgage) and variable expenses (e.g., groceries, entertainment).

2. **Set Clear Financial Goals:**

  - *Short-Term and Long-Term Objectives:* Define your financial goals, both short-term and long-term. Whether it's saving for a vacation, paying off debt, or building an emergency fund, having clear goals shapes your budget.

3. **Categorize Your Spending:**

  - **Fixed vs. Variable Expenses:** Distinguish between fixed and variable expenses. Fixed expenses remain constant, while variable expenses fluctuate. Categorizing helps prioritize and manage these costs effectively.

4. Establish Realistic Categories:

- *Comprehensive Categories:* Create categories that encompass all aspects of your life, including housing, utilities, transportation, groceries, entertainment, and savings. Ensure your categories are comprehensive and reflective of your lifestyle.

5. Determine Your Budgeting Method:

- *Zero-Based Budgeting:* Allocate every dollar of your income to specific expenses, savings, or debt repayment. Aim for a balance of zero at the end, ensuring every dollar has a designated purpose.

- *50/30/20 Rule:* Allocate 50% of your income to needs, 30% to wants, and 20% to savings or debt repayment. This rule provides a simple guideline for budget distribution.

6. Track Your Spending:

- *Record Every Expense:* Keep a record of every expense, whether it's a cup of coffee or a major purchase. Utilize budgeting apps or spreadsheets to streamline the tracking process.

- Regularly Review Transactions: Periodically review your transactions to identify patterns, unnecessary expenditures, or areas where you can cut back.

7. Adjust and Fine-Tune:

- Flexibility for Changes: Life circumstances change, and so should your budget. Be flexible and willing to adjust your budget based on income fluctuations, unexpected expenses, or changes in financial goals.

- Regular Review: Set aside time regularly, such as monthly or quarterly, to review your budget. Ensure that it continues to align with your financial objectives.

8. Prioritize Savings and Debt Repayment:

- Pay Yourself First: Allocate a portion of your income to savings or debt repayment before

addressing other expenses. Prioritizing these categories ensures progress toward financial goals.

- *Emergency Fund:* Include an emergency fund category in your budget to build a financial safety net for unexpected expenses.

9. Celebrate Milestones:

- *Acknowledge Achievements:* Celebrate reaching budgeting milestones or financial goals. Positive reinforcement enhances motivation and encourages continued adherence to your budget.

10. *Seek Professional Guidance:*

- *Financial Advisors:* If needed, consult with financial advisors to refine your budgeting strategy. They can provide personalized advice based on your unique financial situation and goals.

Creating and maintaining a budget that works is an ongoing and dynamic process. It requires diligence, adaptability, and a commitment to financial goals. With a well-crafted budget, individuals can gain control over their finances, make informed decisions, and pave the way to a more secure and prosperous financial future.

- Debt Elimination Strategies for Financial Freedom

Debt elimination is a critical step toward achieving financial freedom, allowing individuals to regain control of their finances and work toward long-term prosperity. Effectively managing and paying off debts requires a strategic approach. Here's a comprehensive discussion of debt elimination strategies for financial freedom:

1. **Assess and Prioritize Debts:**

   - *List All Debts*: Begin by creating a comprehensive list of all your debts, including credit cards, loans, and other outstanding balances.

- Determine Interest Rates: Note the interest rates associated with each debt. Prioritize debts with higher interest rates, as they cost more over time.

2. Create a Debt Repayment Plan:

- Snowball Method: Start with the snowball method, where you pay off the smallest debts first. Once a debt is paid off, roll that payment into the next smallest debt.

- Avalanche Method: Alternatively, use the avalanche method, focusing on debts with the highest interest rates first. This minimizes the overall interest paid.

3. Set a Realistic Budget:

- Review and Adjust Expenses: Analyze your budget to identify areas where you can cut back or reallocate funds toward debt repayment.

- Allocate Windfalls: Allocate unexpected income, tax refunds, or work bonuses toward debt repayment rather than discretionary spending.

4. Negotiate Interest Rates:

 - *Contact Creditors:* Reach out to creditors to negotiate lower interest rates. A lower rate can significantly reduce the overall cost of repaying the debt.

5. Consolidate Debts:

 - *Debt Consolidation Loans:* Consider consolidating high-interest debts into a single, lower-interest loan. This simplifies payments and reduces interest costs.

 - *Balance Transfer Credit Cards:* Transfer high-interest credit card balances to cards with lower introductory rates, but be mindful of transfer fees and the duration of the promotional rate.

6. Explore Debt Settlement:

 - *Negotiate Settlements:* If facing extreme financial hardship, negotiate with creditors for a settlement, where you pay a reduced amount to satisfy the debt. This option may impact your credit score but provides a faster resolution.

7. Generate Additional Income:

  - *Side Hustles and Gig Economy:* Explore opportunities for additional income through side hustles, freelancing, or part-time work. Direct these earnings toward debt repayment.

  - *Sell Unnecessary Assets:* Liquidate assets that are not essential to generate funds for debt repayment.

8. **Seek Professional Assistance:**

  - *Credit Counseling Services:* Enlist the help of credit counselling services. Nonprofit organizations can provide guidance, budgeting assistance, and debt management plans.

  - *Debt Management Plans:* Consider enrolling in a debt management plan (DMP) through a credit counselling agency. DMPs consolidate debts and negotiate with creditors for lower interest rates.

9. **Stay Disciplined and Motivated:**

 - *Celebrate Milestones:* Acknowledge and celebrate small victories along the way. Paying off each debt is an achievement worth recognizing.

 - *Visualize Financial Freedom:* Keep the end goal in mind. Visualize the financial freedom and reduced stress that comes with being debt-free.

10. **Prevent Future Debt Accumulation:**

 - *Build an Emergency Fund:* Establish and maintain an emergency fund to cover unexpected expenses, reducing the need to rely on credit in times of crisis.

 - *Practice Responsible Credit Use:* Learn from past mistakes and adopt responsible credit habits. Use credit wisely and avoid accumulating new debt.

Debt elimination requires commitment, discipline, and strategic planning. By implementing these strategies, individuals can systematically eliminate their debts, regain financial control, and pave the way to long-term financial freedom.

- Emergency Funds and the Power of Financial Resilience

Emergency funds play a pivotal role in fostering financial resilience, providing individuals with a powerful tool to navigate unexpected challenges and uncertainties. In this discussion, we'll explore the significance of emergency funds and how they contribute to the overall power of financial resilience:

1. Creating a Financial Safety Net:

 - *Definition of an Emergency Fund:* An emergency fund is a designated savings account that serves as a financial safety net, specifically earmarked to cover unforeseen expenses or financial emergencies.

 - *Purpose and Function:* The primary function of an emergency fund is to provide a financial cushion, offering peace of mind and a sense of security in the face of unexpected events such as medical emergencies, job loss, or major car repairs.

2. Determining the Size of the Emergency Fund:

- *Rule of Thumb:* Financial experts often recommend saving three to six months' worth of living expenses in an emergency fund. The actual amount can vary based on individual circumstances, such as employment stability, family size, and financial obligations.

- *Assessing Personal Factors:* Consider your specific situation when determining the size of your emergency fund. Factors like job security, industry stability, and the presence of dependents influence the recommended amount.

3. Building the Emergency Fund:

- *Consistent Contributions:* Regularly contribute to your emergency fund, treating it as a non-negotiable monthly expense. Even small contributions can accumulate over time.

- Automated Savings: Set up automatic transfers to your emergency fund to ensure consistent and disciplined savings.

4. Strategic Use of Emergency Funds:

- True Emergencies: Reserve the use of your emergency fund for genuine emergencies, such as unexpected medical expenses, car repairs, or temporary loss of income.

- Avoiding Lifestyle Inflation: Resist the temptation to dip into the fund for non-urgent expenses or lifestyle upgrades. Maintaining its integrity ensures its effectiveness when needed.

5. Financial Resilience beyond Emergencies:

- Adapting to Changes: Financial resilience extends beyond emergencies to adaptability in the face of changes. An emergency fund empowers individuals to navigate life transitions, such as career shifts, without financial strain.

- Reducing Stress: Knowing that you have a financial safety net in place reduces stress and

anxiety associated with unexpected events, allowing for clearer decision-making during challenging times.

6. **Emergency Funds and Debt Prevention:**

- *Preventing Debt Accumulation:* An adequately funded emergency fund acts as a bulwark against accumulating high-interest debt during emergencies. This preventative aspect contributes to long-term financial health.

- *Preserving Financial Goals:* Without the need to rely on credit cards or loans for emergencies, individuals can preserve their financial goals and avoid setbacks in their long-term plans.

7. **Maintaining and Replenishing:**

- *Regular Review:* Periodically review your emergency fund to ensure it remains aligned with your current financial situation. Factors such as changes in income or living expenses may warrant adjustments.

- Replenishing after Use: If you dip into your emergency fund, prioritize replenishing it as soon as possible to maintain its effectiveness for future unforeseen events.

In summary, emergency funds serve as a cornerstone of financial resilience, providing a robust defense against life's unexpected challenges. By diligently building and maintaining an emergency fund, individuals not only gain a sense of financial security but also empower themselves to face uncertainties with confidence and adaptability. The power of financial resilience lies in the ability to weather storms and emerge stronger on the path to long-term financial well-being.

CHAPTER 4: RETIRE EARLY, RETIRE RICH

Welcome to a chapter that ventures beyond conventional timelines and embarks on a journey toward financial liberation – Chapter 4: "Retire Early, Retire Rich." In this section, we delve into the strategies, mindset shifts, and financial man oeuvres that can pave the way to an early retirement without sacrificing wealth or happiness. This chapter is not merely about escaping the workforce ahead of schedule; it's a roadmap to achieving financial independence and basking in the freedom to live life on your terms.

As we immerse ourselves in the world of early retirement, our exploration begins with an understanding of the principles behind the Financial Independence, Retire Early (FIRE) movement. We dissect the core tenets of frugality, strategic investing, and intentional living that have empowered individuals to break free from the traditional retirement age constraints.

Following this, we navigate the landscape of Smart Investment Strategies for Early Retirement. From optimizing asset allocation to harnessing the power of compounding, this section provides insights into building a robust investment portfolio that sustains your desired lifestyle beyond the traditional retirement age.

Our journey culminates in Lifestyle Design for Early Retirees, where we unravel the art of crafting a purposeful and fulfilling post-retirement life. From travel adventures to pursuing passions and meaningful endeavors, this section explores how early retirees can cultivate a life rich in experiences and personal fulfilment.

Get ready to explore a paradigm shift in retirement planning. "Retire Early, Retire Rich" is not just a chapter; it's an invitation to reimagine your relationship with work, money, and time. It's a blueprint for those who aspire to break free from conventional constraints and embrace a future where financial independence and early retirement coalesce to create a life of abundance and fulfilment. Let the journey toward early retirement, enriched with wisdom and strategic insights, commence.

- Crafting a Personalized Early Retirement Plan

Crafting a personalized early retirement plan is a strategic and thoughtful process that involves careful consideration of your financial goals, lifestyle preferences, and risk tolerance. Achieving early retirement requires a comprehensive approach that includes saving diligently, investing wisely, and making intentional choices to align your finances with your desired lifestyle. Here's a detailed discussion of the process:

1. **Define Your Retirement Goals:**

   - Clarity on Lifestyle: Clearly articulate the lifestyle you envision during early retirement.

Consider factors such as travel, hobbies, housing, and healthcare to estimate the financial requirements.

- *Retirement Age:* Determine the age at which you aim to retire. This establishes the time horizon for your early retirement plan.

2. Assess Your Current Financial Situation:

- *Net worth Calculation:* Evaluate your current net worth by assessing assets and liabilities. This snapshot provides a baseline for your early retirement planning.

- *Income and Expenses:* Analyze your current income and expenses to understand your saving capacity. Identify areas where you can increase savings to accelerate your early retirement timeline.

3. Estimate Early Retirement Expenses:

- *Detailed Budgeting:* Create a detailed budget that accounts for all expected expenses during early retirement. Include categories such as healthcare, travel, leisure activities, and any other lifestyle preferences.

   - *Inflation Considerations:* Factor in inflation when estimating future expenses to ensure your plan remains realistic over time.

4. Determine Retirement Income Sources:

   - *Passive Income:* Identify potential sources of passive income, such as investments, rental income, or royalties. Passive income streams contribute to financial stability during retirement.

   - *Social Security and Pensions:* Consider the impact of Social Security benefits or any pensions you may be eligible for, even if you retire early.

5. Create a Tax-Efficient Strategy:

   - *Tax-Advantaged Accounts:* Maximize contributions to tax-advantaged retirement accounts like 401(k)s and IRAs. Understand the tax implications of withdrawals during early retirement.

- Tax Planning: Craft a tax-efficient withdrawal strategy to minimize tax liabilities during early retirement.

6. **Optimize Investment Strategies:**

- Asset Allocation: Define an asset allocation strategy that aligns with your risk tolerance and retirement goals. Consider a diversified portfolio that balances growth and stability.

- Withdrawal Strategies: Plan for a sustainable withdrawal strategy that ensures your portfolio lasts throughout early retirement. Strategies such as the 4% rule may be considered.

7. **Emergency Fund and Contingency Planning:**

- Maintain an Emergency Fund: Preserve or establish an emergency fund to cover unforeseen expenses, ensuring that unexpected events don't derail your early retirement plans.

- Healthcare Contingency: Develop a plan for healthcare coverage during early retirement, considering options such as Health Savings

Accounts (HSAs) and budgeting for potential healthcare expenses.

8. Regularly Review and Adjust the Plan:

- *Periodic Assessments:* Regularly review your early retirement plan to ensure it remains aligned with your goals. Consider adjustments based on changes in your financial situation, market conditions, or personal preferences.

- *Flexibility:* Incorporate flexibility into your plan to adapt to unexpected changes or opportunities.

9. Consider Risk Management:

- *Insurance Coverage:* Evaluate your insurance coverage, including health, life, and long-term care insurance. Adequate coverage protects against unforeseen risks that could impact your early retirement.

10. Seek Professional Advice:

- *Financial Advisor Consultation:* Consider seeking advice from a financial advisor specializing in early retirement planning. A professional can provide personalized insights and guidance tailored to your specific situation.

Crafting a personalized early retirement plan is an ongoing and dynamic process. By systematically addressing these components and staying attuned to your financial landscape, you can work towards achieving the dream of early retirement while maintaining financial security and sustainability throughout your post-employment years.

- Maximizing Retirement Accounts and Benefits

Maximizing retirement accounts and benefits is a crucial aspect of effective retirement planning. By optimizing contributions to tax-advantaged accounts and strategically leveraging available benefits, individuals can enhance their retirement savings and create a more secure financial future. Here's a detailed discussion of the process:

1. **Understand Available Retirement Accounts:**

- **401(k):** If offered by your employer, contribute to your 401(k) account. Take advantage of employer matching contributions, as they represent free money added to your retirement savings.

- *IRA (Individual Retirement Account):* Contribute to an IRA, either traditional or Roth, depending on your tax situation and retirement goals. IRAs offer tax advantages and a range of investment options.

2. **Contribute Up to the Maximum Allowance:**

- **401(k) Contribution Limits:** Stay informed about annual contribution limits for 401(k) accounts. Contribute the maximum allowable amount, adjusting your contributions each year to account for changes in limits.

- *IRA Contribution Limits:* Similarly, be aware of contribution limits for IRAs. Contribute up to the maximum allowable amount to benefit from tax advantages and compound growth.

3. Take Advantage of Catch-Up Contributions:

 - Age 50 and Older: Individuals aged 50 and older are eligible for catch-up contributions. This allows for higher contribution limits in both 401(k)s and IRAs. Leverage this opportunity to accelerate retirement savings in the later stages of your career.

4. **Consider Employer Matching Contributions:**

 - *Maximize Employer Matching:* If your employer offers a matching contribution to your 401(k), contribute enough to maximize this benefit. Employer matching represents an immediate return on investment and boosts your overall retirement savings.

5. **Diversify Between Pre-Tax and Roth Contributions:**

 - *401(k) vs. Roth 401(k):* Some employers offer Roth 401(k) options. Consider diversifying between traditional (pre-tax) and Roth (after-tax) contributions to provide flexibility in managing future tax liabilities during retirement.

6. Review and Adjust Investment Allocations:

- *Regular Portfolio Reviews:* Periodically review and adjust your investment allocations within retirement accounts. Ensure that your portfolio aligns with your risk tolerance, time horizon, and retirement goals.

7. Utilize Health Savings Accounts (HSAs):

- *Triple Tax Advantages:* If eligible, contribute to a Health Savings Account (HSA). HSAs offer triple tax advantages: contributions are tax-deductible, earnings grow tax-free, and withdrawals for qualified medical expenses are tax-free.

8. Optimize Social Security Benefits:

- *Delaying Social Security:* Delaying the start of Social Security benefits can result in higher monthly payments. Assess your financial situation and health to determine the optimal time to start receiving Social Security.

9. Explore Other Employer-Sponsored Benefits:

- *Employer Pension Plans:* If your employer offers a pension plan, understand how it works and take advantage of it. Pension plans provide additional sources of retirement income.

- *Stock Purchase Plans:* Participate in employer stock purchase plans if available. These programs may offer discounted stock prices and a convenient way to build additional wealth.

10. Stay Informed About Tax Law Changes:

- *Tax Law Considerations:* Stay abreast of changes in tax laws that may impact retirement accounts. Adjust your strategies accordingly to maximize tax advantages and optimize your overall financial plan.

11. Seek Professional Guidance:

- *Financial Advisor Consultation:* Consider consulting with a financial advisor to tailor your retirement strategy to your unique situation.

Professional guidance can help you make informed decisions and navigate complex financial scenarios.

Maximizing retirement accounts and benefits involves a combination of proactive planning, ongoing adjustments, and strategic decision-making. By leveraging available tax-advantaged accounts, optimizing contributions, and staying informed about retirement benefits, individuals can build a robust financial foundation for a secure and fulfilling retirement.

- Balancing Risk and Reward in Your Investment Portfolio

Balancing risk and reward in your investment portfolio is a critical aspect of prudent and effective investment management. Achieving an equilibrium that aligns with your financial goals, risk tolerance, and time horizon requires thoughtful planning and strategic decision-making. Here's a comprehensive discussion of the process:

1. Define Your Financial Goals:

 - *Short-Term vs. Long-Term Goals:* Clearly articulate your financial goals, distinguishing between short-term objectives (e.g., buying a house) and long-term goals (e.g., retirement). Your goals will influence the level of risk you can afford to take.

2. Assess Your Risk Tolerance:

 - *Risk Tolerance Questionnaire:* Use risk tolerance assessments or questionnaires to evaluate your comfort level with investment risk. Understand that risk tolerance can vary among individuals and may change over time.

3. Understand Different Types of Risk:

 - *Market Risk:* The potential for investment losses due to market fluctuations.

 - *Credit Risk:* The risk of default by bond issuers or borrowers.

- *Inflation Risk:* The impact of inflation eroding the purchasing power of your investments.

- *Liquidity Risk:* The risk of being unable to sell an investment quickly without significantly impacting its price.

4. Diversify Your Portfolio:

- *Asset Allocation:* Diversify your investments across different asset classes, such as stocks, bonds, and real estate. Asset allocation helps spread risk and can enhance portfolio stability.

- *Geographic Diversification:* Consider diversifying globally to reduce exposure to regional economic risks.

5. Invest According to Your Time Horizon:

- *Short-Term vs. Long-Term Investments:* Align your investment choices with your time horizon. Long-term goals may tolerate more volatility, allowing for a higher allocation to growth-oriented assets like stocks.

6. Consider Your Age and Stage of Life:

- *Life Stage Considerations:* Younger investors may have a longer time horizon and can generally afford to take on more risk. As you approach retirement, a more conservative approach to risk may be appropriate to preserve capital.

7. Balancing Equities and Fixed Income:

- *Stocks vs. Bonds:* Equities (stocks) typically offer higher potential returns but come with higher volatility. Bonds, on the other hand, provide income and stability. Balancing the mix based on your risk tolerance is crucial.

8. Rebalance Regularly:

- *Periodic Portfolio Review:* Regularly review your investment portfolio to ensure it remains in line with your target asset allocation. Rebalance by buying or selling assets to bring the portfolio back to its intended mix.

9. Consider Alternative Investments:

- *Diversification with Alternatives:* Explore alternative investments like real estate, commodities, or private equity to further diversify your portfolio. These assets may behave differently than traditional stocks and bonds.

10. Stay Informed and Monitor Economic Trends:

- *Market Research:* Keep abreast of economic and market trends. Understand how global events and economic indicators may impact your investments.

- *Professional Advice:* Consider seeking advice from financial professionals who can provide insights into market conditions and help adjust your portfolio as needed.

11. Use Risk Management Strategies:

- *Stop-Loss Orders:* Implement stop-loss orders to automatically sell an investment if it reaches a predetermined price, limiting potential losses.

- Hedging Strategies: Explore hedging strategies, such as options or futures, to mitigate downside risk in your portfolio.

12. Review and Adjust as Needed:

- Life Changes and Market Conditions: Life events, changes in income, or shifts in market conditions may necessitate adjustments to your risk and reward strategy. Be prepared to adapt your portfolio accordingly.

13. Distinguish Between Speculation and Investment:

- Speculative vs. Investment Positions: Clearly distinguish between speculative positions and long-term investments. Speculative ventures may offer higher potential returns but also carry higher risk.

Balancing risk and reward is an ongoing process that requires vigilance and adaptability. By understanding your financial goals, risk tolerance, and the dynamics of your investments, you can construct a well-balanced portfolio that seeks to optimize returns while managing risk effectively.

Regular review, diversification, and a thoughtful approach to asset allocation contribute to a resilient and well-rounded investment strategy.

CHAPTER 5: BEYOND WEALTH: CULTIVATING HAPPINESS AND FULFILLMENT

Welcome to a chapter that transcends the traditional narrative of financial success and ventures into the profound realm of personal contentment – Chapter 5: "Beyond Wealth: Cultivating Happiness and Fulfillment." In this transformative section, we embark on a journey that extends beyond the balance sheets and investment portfolios, exploring the facets of life that contribute to genuine happiness and lasting fulfilment.

As we delve into the exploration of what lies "Beyond Wealth," our focus shifts from monetary metrics to the more intangible and enriching aspects of existence. This chapter invites you to ponder essential questions about the purpose of wealth, the pursuit of passions, and the significance of meaningful relationships.

Our exploration begins with the concept of a Holistic Definition of Success. Beyond financial achievements, we consider success as a multifaceted jewel that encompasses personal growth, contribution to society, and the pursuit of endeavors that bring joy and purpose. The pursuit of happiness and fulfilment is not a destination but a continuous journey of self-discovery and enrichment.

Following this, we unravel the importance of Gratitude and Mindfulness in fostering contentment. In a world often preoccupied with the next milestone, cultivating gratitude and being present at the moment emerge as powerful practices that enhance overall well-being. We delve into actionable strategies to incorporate gratitude and mindfulness into your daily life.

Our journey into "Beyond Wealth" culminates in the exploration of the Impact of Giving Back. Whether through acts of kindness, philanthropy, or community engagement, contributing to the well-being of others has a profound effect on one's sense of purpose and fulfilment. This section provides insights into how giving back can become a cornerstone of a truly rich and meaningful life.

Get ready to transcend the conventional notions of success and wealth. "Beyond Wealth: Cultivating Happiness and Fulfillment" is not just a chapter; it's an invitation to reflect on the essence of a life well-lived. It's an exploration of the intangible qualities that define true prosperity and leave a lasting legacy. Let the journey toward genuine happiness and fulfilment unfold, enriching your perspective and guiding you toward a life of purpose and joy.

- The Role of Money in a Happy Life

The role of money in a happy life is a complex and multifaceted aspect of individual well-being. While money is undoubtedly a tool that can enhance various aspects of life, its influence on happiness is nuanced and extends beyond material wealth. Here are key points to consider when examining the role of money in a happy life:

1. Basic Needs and Security:

- Money plays a fundamental role in meeting basic needs such as food, shelter, and healthcare. Having financial security and meeting these essential requirements contributes significantly to overall well-being.

2. Byond Basic Needs:

- Once basic needs are met, the correlation between money and happiness diminishes. Studies suggest that incremental increases in income have diminishing returns in terms of happiness beyond a certain threshold.

3. Quality of Life:

- Money can contribute to an improved quality of life by providing access to education, healthcare, and leisure activities. It enables individuals to enjoy experiences and opportunities that enhance life satisfaction.

4. Freedom and Choices:

- Financial resources provide individuals with the freedom to make choices that align with their values and preferences. This may include pursuing education, travelling, or engaging in hobbies that bring joy.

5. Diminishing Marginal Utility:

- The concept of diminishing marginal utility suggests that as income increases, the additional happiness derived from each additional dollar decreases. Beyond a certain point, the pursuit of wealth may not significantly contribute to overall happiness.

6. Comparison and Social Influence:

- Social comparison and the influence of societal norms can impact perceptions of happiness. The desire for material possessions or a certain lifestyle driven by societal expectations can create a perpetual cycle of striving for more, potentially undermining contentment.

7. Financial Stress and Unhappiness:

- Financial stress, debt, and insecurity can have a detrimental impact on mental health and overall well-being. Managing finances responsibly and having a plan can mitigate stress and contribute to a happier life.

8. Personal Values and Fulfillment:

- Happiness is deeply tied to a sense of purpose, personal values, and fulfilment. Pursuing activities and goals aligned with one's values, rather than purely monetary pursuits, is often a more reliable source of lasting happiness.

9. Social Connections:

- Strong social connections and relationships are consistently associated with happiness. While money can facilitate social activities and connections, the quality of relationships plays a more significant role in long-term happiness.

10. Philanthropy and Giving:

- Research indicates that spending money on others, whether through acts of kindness or philanthropy, can contribute to a sense of purpose and joy. Acts of generosity can provide a deeper sense of fulfilment than personal consumption.

11. Mindset and Adaptation:

- The concept of hedonic adaptation suggests that individuals tend to adapt to changes in circumstances, including income increases. This adaptation may limit the sustained impact of financial improvements on happiness over time.

In summary, while money is undeniably important for meeting basic needs and providing opportunities, its role in overall happiness is complex. The pursuit of a happy life involves a balance between meeting essential needs, making choices aligned with personal values, fostering social connections, and finding fulfilment beyond material possessions. A holistic approach to well-being considers the interplay of financial resources with personal values, relationships, and a sense of purpose.

- Pursuing Passions: Turning Hobbies into Income

Pursuing passions and turning hobbies into income is a gratifying journey that allows individuals to blend their interests with entrepreneurial spirit. This process involves a thoughtful transition from enjoying a hobby to creating a sustainable source of income. Here's a detailed discussion of the steps involved:

1. **Identify Your Passion:**

- *Self-Reflection:* Identify hobbies and activities that genuinely bring you joy and fulfilment. Consider the skills and knowledge you have developed in these areas.

2. **Assess Market Demand:**

- *Market Research:* Evaluate the market demand for products or services related to your passion. Identify potential customers, competitors, and trends within the niche.

3. **Define Your Niche:**

- *Specialization:* Define a niche within your passion that allows you to stand out. Specialization can attract a dedicated audience and make your offerings unique.

4. Develop Skills and Expertise:

- *Continuous Learning:* Invest time in developing and enhancing your skills related to your passion. Stay informed about industry trends, techniques, and innovations.

5. Create a Business Plan:

- *Define Objectives:* Clearly outline your business objectives, target audience, revenue streams, and marketing strategy in a comprehensive business plan.

- *Financial Projections:* Include financial projections, outlining how you plan to generate income and cover expenses.

6. Build an Online Presence:

- *Website and Social Media:* Establish a professional online presence through a website and social media platforms. Showcase your passion, skills, and offerings to attract potential customers.

7. Monetize Your Passion:

- *Products or Services:* Determine how to monetize your passion. This could involve selling products, offering services, conducting workshops, or providing consultations.

- *Multiple Revenue Streams:* Explore multiple revenue streams, such as merchandise sales, online courses, memberships, or affiliate marketing.

8. Set Realistic Goals:

- *Short-Term and Long-Term Goals:* Set achievable short-term goals and long-term milestones. This helps maintain focus and provides a roadmap for the growth of your passion-based business.

9. Test the Waters:

- *Pilot Projects:* Before fully committing, test your business concept through pilot projects, beta launches, or small-scale offerings. Gather feedback and make necessary adjustments.

10. **Establish a Pricing Strategy:**

- *Competitive Pricing:* Research pricing strategies in your niche. Ensure that your pricing is competitive while reflecting the value you provide.

11. **Network and Collaborate:**

- *Networking:* Build relationships within your industry. Attend events, join online communities, and collaborate with other professionals to expand your network and opportunities.

12. **Invest in Marketing:**

- *Digital Marketing:* Invest in digital marketing strategies such as social media marketing, content creation, and email campaigns. Use platforms to showcase your passion and connect with your audience.

13. **Manage Finances Effectively:**

- *Budgeting:* Implement effective financial management. Keep track of income and expenses, and allocate resources strategically to support business growth.

14. Customer Engagement and Feedback:

- Customer Relationship Management: Foster strong relationships with your customers. Encourage feedback and use it to improve your products or services.

15. Adapt and Evolve:

- Flexibility: Stay flexible and open to evolving your business based on market trends, customer feedback, and changes in your interests.

16. Legal Considerations:

- Business Structure and Compliance: Choose an appropriate business structure and ensure compliance with legal requirements. This includes registering your business, obtaining necessary licenses, and addressing tax obligations.

17. Work-Life Balance:

- Set Boundaries: Maintain a healthy work-life balance. Define clear boundaries to prevent burnout and ensure that your passion remains a source of joy.

Turning hobbies into income is a rewarding venture that requires a combination of passion, business acumen, and strategic planning. By approaching the process thoughtfully and leveraging available resources, individuals can transform their passions into fulfilling and sustainable income-generating endeavors.

- Achieving Work-Life Balance and Sustainable Happiness

Achieving work-life balance and sustainable happiness is a dynamic process that involves intentional efforts to harmonize professional responsibilities with personal well-being. Striking the right equilibrium contributes to overall life satisfaction, mental health, and sustained happiness. Here's a detailed discussion of the process:

1. Define Your Priorities:

- *Identify Core Values:* Reflect on your core values and priorities in both your professional and personal life. Clarify what matters most to you.

2. Set Clear Boundaries:

- *Work Boundaries:* Establish clear boundaries between work and personal life. Define specific working hours and avoid extending work into personal time whenever possible.

3. Prioritize Self-Care:

- *Physical Health:* Prioritize regular exercise, a balanced diet, and sufficient sleep. Physical well-being forms the foundation for overall happiness.

- *Mental Health:* Incorporate practices that support mental health, such as mindfulness, meditation, or engaging in activities that bring joy and relaxation.

4. **Effective Time Management:**

- *Prioritization:* Use effective time management techniques to prioritize tasks based on importance and deadlines. This helps prevent feeling overwhelmed and allows for better focus on high-priority activities.

5. **Learn to Say No:**

- *Set Boundaries at Work:* Be willing to say no to additional work commitments when you are at capacity. Communicate your limitations and ensure a realistic workload.

6. **Establish a Routine:**

- *Consistent Schedule:* Establish a consistent daily or weekly routine that accommodates both work and personal activities. Routine provides structure and predictability.

7. **Utilize Technology Wisely:**

- *Digital Detox:* Schedule regular digital detox periods to disconnect from work-related devices.

Use technology mindfully to enhance efficiency rather than letting it intrude on personal time.

8. *Flexible Work Arrangements:*

- *Explore Flexibility:* If possible, explore flexible work arrangements, such as remote work or flexible hours. Negotiate with employers to find a balance that meets both personal and professional needs.

9. **Quality over Quantity:**

- *Focus on Productivity:* Emphasize productivity over the number of hours worked. Efficient work habits allow for a more streamlined approach, freeing up time for personal pursuits.

10. **Invest in Relationships:**

- *Family and Friends:* Cultivate meaningful relationships with family and friends. Allocate dedicated time for social connections to nurture a support system.

11. Regular Reflection:

- Assess and Adjust: Regularly reflect on your work-life balance and happiness. Assess what is working well and what adjustments may be necessary to align with changing circumstances.

12. Set Realistic Goals:

- Achievable Targets: Establish realistic and achievable goals in both professional and personal domains. Setting overly ambitious goals can contribute to stress and imbalance.

13. Delegate Responsibilities:

- Effective Delegation: Delegate tasks at work and share household responsibilities. Acknowledge that seeking support is a sign of strength, not weakness.

14. Continuous Learning:

- Adaptability: Embrace a mindset of continuous learning and adaptability. Be open to refining your approach to work and life based on new insights and experiences.

15. Celebrate Achievements:

- *Acknowledge Milestones:* Celebrate both professional and personal achievements. Taking time to acknowledge accomplishments reinforces a sense of fulfilment.

16. Seek Professional Support:

- *Therapy or Counseling:* If work-related stress or personal challenges become overwhelming, consider seeking the support of a therapist or counsellor. Professional guidance can provide valuable insights.

17. Regularly Disconnect:

- *Scheduled Breaks:* Schedule regular breaks and vacations to fully disconnect from work. Engage in activities that rejuvenate and bring joy during these breaks.

18. Define Success on Your Terms:

- *Personal Definition:* Rethink your definition of success. Strive for a definition that aligns with your values rather than societal expectations.

19. Continuous Communication:

- Communication with Others: Maintain open communication with family members, colleagues, and friends. Discuss your goals and boundaries, ensuring a shared understanding.

20. Evolve and Adapt:

- Life Stages: Recognize that work-life balance evolves with different life stages and circumstances. Be willing to adapt your strategies to accommodate changing priorities.

Achieving work-life balance and sustainable happiness is an ongoing process that requires self-awareness, adaptability, and conscious decision-making. By prioritizing well-being, setting boundaries, and fostering meaningful connections, individuals can create a fulfilling and sustainable life that encompasses both personal and professional aspects.

CONCLUSION

As we reach the culmination of "Financial Freedom: How to Retire Young, Rich, and Happy," I extend my heartfelt gratitude for joining me on this transformative journey toward a life of abundance and fulfilment. Throughout these pages, we've explored the profound intersections of financial wisdom, personal happiness, and the pursuit of a purposeful existence.

Our odyssey began by redefining the very essence of wealth, moving beyond mere financial prosperity to embrace a holistic understanding of abundance that encompasses joy, passion, and meaningful connections. We unraveled the intricacies of building a robust financial foundation, crafting an investment strategy that balances risk and reward, and navigating the intricacies of passive income streams.

The chapters guided us through the psychology of money, the art of wealth accumulation, and the strategic avenues of smart saving and investing. We delved into the realms of debt elimination, emergency funds, and the indispensable power of financial resilience. With each revelation, the path to financial freedom became clearer, more attainable, and uniquely personal.

But our expedition was not confined to numbers and spreadsheets. It extended into the intangible landscapes of happiness and purpose. We explored the significance of cultivating gratitude, mindfulness, and the immeasurable impact of giving back. We transcended the conventional boundaries of success, stepping into a realm where wealth becomes a means to a greater end – a life rich in experiences, relationships, and profound fulfilment.

As we bid farewell to this journey, I encourage you to carry forth the wisdom gained in your pursuit of financial freedom. May these insights empower you to navigate the complexities of personal finance, embrace a mindset of abundance, and chart a course toward a retirement that is not merely an escape from work but a leap into a life of extraordinary richness.

Remember, the essence of financial freedom lies not just in retiring young, rich, and happy, but in savouring each step of the journey, relishing the moments, and finding joy in the pursuit of your passions. Your financial freedom is a tool – a tool to create a life that aligns with your deepest desires and resonates with the truest version of yourself.

As you close this book, may you embark on your odyssey toward a future where wealth and happiness intertwine, leading you to a retirement that is not an end but a glorious beginning – a new chapter where you are the author of a life well-lived, abundant in prosperity, purpose, and enduring joy.